P9-EJZ-113

DO THE RIGHT THING!

SHARING

Written by Chip Lovitt
Illustrated by Anne Thornburgh

ROURKE BOOK CO, INC.
VERO BEACH, FL 32964

Printed in the United States of America.

Library of Congress Cataloging-in-Publication Data

Lovitt Chip.
   Sharing / Chip Lovitt.
      p.   cm. — (Doing the right thing)
Summary: Simple text and illustrations provide examples of sharing in everyday life.
   ISBN 1-55916-236-8
   1. Sharing—Juvenile literature. [1. Sharing.]   I. Title.
II. Series.
BJ1533.G4L68   1999
177′.7—dc21

                                      98-48387
                                           CIP
                                           AC

SHARING

Do you know what sharing is?

Sharing is inviting your friends to your house and letting them play with your favorite toys.

Enjoying a plate of delicious chocolate chip cookies with your friends is sharing. It is fun when everybody gets a cookie, or two.

Sharing is lending your best friend a cool
T-shirt when he gets his wet running
through the sprinkler on a hot afternoon.

Sharing is enjoying a joke
or funny story together.

Sharing is letting your best friend ride your brand new bike, even though you might be a little worried that it will get scratched.

Sharing is giving your best friend a piece of candy, even when it is the last one in the box.

Sharing is lending a classmate one of your pencils when she needs one.

When you and a friend share your
favorite music CDs or tapes for the
week, both of you get to hear twice
as much music.

Letting everyone have their turn on
the swings is a nice way to share fun
in the park.

Sharing is letting your little brother
play your video game, even though he
is not very good at it.

Sharing is letting your sister watch her favorite TV show, even though you would rather watch another show.

Spending a special moment with someone is
sharing. Reading a bedtime story to your
baby sister is a nice thing to do. She cannot
read yet, but you can share a story together.

Teamwork is all about sharing, and it makes a team better. Sharing is letting one of your teammates take a last-minute shot, even though you could have taken the shot yourself.

21

Sharing is letting your teammates
use your brand new baseball bat.

The whole team shares the excitement when one of your teammates gets the game-winning hit with your bat.

Sharing is bringing cupcakes to school
on your birthday.

24

Mother's Day is extra special when you share your feelings. Making a homemade card or gift for your mother helps everybody enjoy a happy event even more.

You can share your time too. It is always nice to spend a day with your grandparents.

Sharing is helping your parents with chores
around the house. It is easier when everyone
does their fair share.

Sharing your time and strength by helping
a neighbor makes you feel good.

Sharing is lending a hand when an important job needs to be done.

Sharing is about giving. When you
share with others, they share with you.
Sharing makes everyone feel good.

You Can Share!

These steps can help you share with others. But do NOT write in this book; use a sheet a paper.

1. **Choose what you can share.** Write 6 things.

   Write 3 things you own, like these:

a game	a soccer ball	a skateboard
stickers	a pencil	a lunch

   Write 3 things you can do, like these:

tell jokes	take walks	mail letters
smile	draw pictures	call on phone

2. **Choose who you can share with.** Write 6 real names.

brother	mom	grandfather	teacher
cousin	neighbor	kid at school	aunt

3. **Choose what to share with each person.** Draw a line from each thing to a name.

   a game ------------------------- little brother
   tell jokes ----------------------- mom
   a lunch -------------------------- kid at school
   draw pictures ------------------ grandfather

4. **Choose to start now.** Share something before you go to bed tonight.

5. **Choose to share each day.** Think about sharing soon after you get out of bed.

6. **Write these words every evening:**
   Today I shared _____ with _____.
   Fill in the blanks. Use the same paper every time. Keep it up for 2 weeks or more.

7. **Say, "I'm generous (JEN er us). I share."**
   Say it many times every day.